DRIVER'S PRACTICE HANDBOOK

NEW EDITION

Preface

According to the new written permit test, to pass the exam, you must obtain more than 85% of correct answers. A correct answer can include several elements of an answer.

Use this book as a practical guide to prepare for the knowledge test that all new drivers must pass to obtain their provisional license.

About 50% of those who take the knowledge test fail it the first time.
So, be sure:

Before You Use This Book

- First, study the official manual of your local government Department of Motor Vehicles to gain fundamental knowledge (free to download from the official website).
- Second, use this book to practice and test your knowledge by answering a variety of questions you may encounter on exam day.

Some questions from the new exam appeal to the behavior, situations, and your ability to use common sense. This book offers many questions with answers.
Questions can be more advanced than others and can also apply to CDL exam.

How to Use This Book

You can go through this book from beginning to end and answer question-by-question to identify your strengths and weaknesses. Identify any questions that you have answered incorrectly and focus on understanding the questions as well as the answers.

Alternatively, you can have another person read the questions aloud to you and correct any wrong answers. Questions in this book span subjects from all chapters in the DMV manual.

For your convenience, answers in this book are written in small font below each question

ROAD SIGNS
Questions and Answers

1) When you see this sign and shape in red color, you must:

A. Stop completely, check for pedestrians, and cross traffic
B. Slow down without coming to a complete stop
C. Stop completely and wait for a green light
D. Slow down and check for traffic

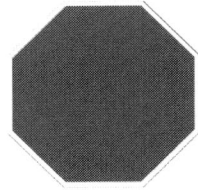

Correct Answer is a

2) This is the shape of a _____ sign.

A. Stop
B. Wrong way
C. Yield
D. Do not enter

Correct Answer is c

3) This sign in red means:

A. Stop
B. No U-turn
C. Yield
D. Do not enter

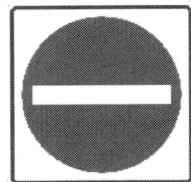

Correct Answer is d

4) This sign means:

A. No U-turn
B. No turning
C. No left turn
D. No right turn

Correct Answer is a

5) This sign means:

A. No U-turn
B. No left turn
C. No right turn
D. No turning

Correct Answer is c

6) This sign means:

A. You must turn left or right
B. You are approaching a t-intersection
C. The road that you are on intersects with a divided highway
D. Designates an overpass above a divided highway

DIVIDED
HIGHWAY

Correct Answer is c

7) You need to use extra caution when driving near a pedestrian using a white cane because:

    A. He or she is deaf
    B. He or she has a mental disability
    C. He or she is blind
    D. He or she has a walking problem

Correct Answer is c

8) When driving near a blind pedestrian who is carrying a white cane or using a guide dog, you should:

    A. Slow down and be prepared to stop
    B. Take the right-of-way
    C. Proceed normally
    D. Drive away quickly

Correct Answer is a

9) If there are no signals at a railroad crossing, you should:

    A. Slow down and prepare to stop if you see or hear a train approaching
    B. Proceed as quickly as possible over the tracks
    C. Proceed through the crossing at a normal rate
    D. Proceed slowly over the tracks

Correct Answer is a

10) You may drive around the gates at a railroad crossing:

A. When the train has passed
B. Never
C. When the lights have stopped flashing
D. When other drivers drive around the gates

Correct Answer is b

11) If you see this sign above your lane, you:

A. May not exit the freeway in this lane
B. May continue through the interchange or exit the freeway in this lane
C. May stay in this lane and continue through the interchange
D. Must exit the freeway if you stay in this lane

EXIT 30-W

22 WEST
Progress
1 MILE

EXIT ↓ ONLY

Correct Answer is d

12) Highway and expressway guide signs are:

A. Orange with black letters
B. Green with white letters
C. Yellow with black letters
D. Red with white letters

Correct Answer is b

13) This sign with a yellow background is used to warn drivers about:

A. Upcoming intersections
B. Road construction
C. Road curves ahead
D. Changes in traffic lanes

Correct Answer is c

14) This sign with a yellow background tells you that:

A. No turns are allowed on this road
B. The road narrows ahead
C. There are a series of curves ahead
D. The road may be slippery when wet

Correct Answer is c

15) This sign with a yellow background means:

A. Left curve ahead
B. Series of curves
C. S curved ahead
D. Slippery when wet

Correct Answer is d

16) This sign with a yellow background indicates that:

A. There is a steep hill ahead
B. No trucks are allowed on the hill
C. A logging road is ahead
D. There are trucks on the hill

17) A yellow and black diamond-shaped sign:

A. Warns you about conditions on or near the road
B. Helps direct you to cities and towns ahead
C. Tells you about traffic laws and regulations
D. Tells you about road construction ahead

18) The sign with this shape in yellow color is a _____ sign.

A. No passing zone
B. Wrong way
C. Railroad crossing
D. Stop

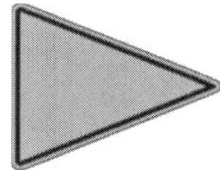

19) Which of these signs is used to show the end of a divided highway?

A. 2
B. 4
C. 3
D. 1

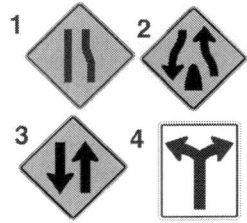

20) This sign with a yellow background is used to warn drivers about:

A. Lane ends, merge left
B. Road curves ahead
C. Upcoming intersections
D. Road construction

21) This sign with a yellow background shows one type of:

A. Intersection
B. Road curve
C. Right turn
D. Lane change

22) This sign with a yellow background shows one type of:

    A. Right turn
    B. Intersection
    C. Lane change
    D. Road curve

Correct Answer is b

23) What should you be most concerned about when you see this sign?

    A. Driving with your headlights out of alignment because one side of your car is higher than the other
    B. Damaging a tire if you drift onto the shoulder
    C. Hydroplaning, if the shoulder has water on it
    D. Losing control of your vehicle, if you drift onto the shoulder, because of a drop off

Correct Answer is d

24) What is the meaning of this sign?

    A. The traffic signal ahead is red
    B. The traffic signal ahead is broken
    C. The traffic signal ahead is green
    D. There is a traffic signal ahead

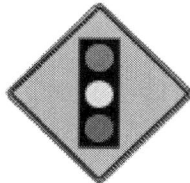

Correct Answer is d

25) This sign with a yellow background means:

A. Divided highway ends
B. One-way street begins
C. One-way street ends
D. Divided highway begins

Correct Answer is d

26) From top to bottom, the following is the proper order for traffic lights:

A. Red, yellow, green
B. Red, green, yellow
C. Green, red, yellow
D. Green, yellow, red

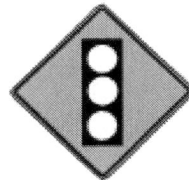

Correct Answer is a

27) If a green arrow turns into a green light, you:

A. May still turn but you must yield to oncoming traffic
B. May no longer turn and must proceed straight
C. Still have the right of way to turn
D. No longer have to turn the way the arrow indicates

Correct Answer is a

28) A steady yellow light at an intersection means:

A. Go
B. Yield to other cars
C. Slow down and prepare to stop
D. Stop

Correct Answer is c

29) A flashing yellow light means that you should:

A. Slow down and proceed with care
B. Continue through if the way is clear
C. Stop and proceed when a green light appears
D. Stop and proceed when the way is clear

Correct Answer is a

30) You must stop when you see a:

A. Flashing red light
B. Steady yellow light
C. Yellow arrow
D. Flashing yellow light

Correct Answer is a

31) A steady green light at an intersection means that you:

A. Must slow down and prepare to stop
B. Must stop and check for oncoming traffic before proceeding
C. May drive through the intersection if the road is clear
D. May not turn right

Correct Answer is c

32) A steady yellow light means that a _____ light will soon appear.

A. Flashing yellow
B. Steady green
C. Steady red
D. Flashing red

Correct Answer is c

33) You may continue carefully through a yellow light if:

A. There is an emergency vehicle crossing your lane
B. There are no pedestrians crossing
C. You are turning right
D. You are within the intersection

Correct Answer is d

34) You may turn left at a red light if:

A. There is no traffic coming in the opposite direction
B. You are turning from a two-way street onto a one-way street
C. You are turning from a one-way street onto another one-way street
D. The car in front of you turns left

Correct Answer is c

35) If a traffic light is broken or not functioning you should:

A. Stop and wait for it to be repaired
B. Stop and wait for a police officer to arrive
C. Continue as if it were a four-way stop sign
D. Continue as you normally would

Correct Answer is c

36) You may turn right on red if you:

A. Stop first and check for traffic and pedestrians
B. Have a right turn red arrow
C. Are in the left lane
D. Slow down first

Correct Answer is a

37) When making a right turn on a green light, you must:

A. Maintain normal driving speed
B. Stop and look for oncoming traffic
C. Yield to pedestrians
D. Increase your normal driving speed

Correct Answer is c

38) The speed limit is _____ miles per hour when the yellow lights are flashing on the school zone speed sign.

A. 25
B. 15
C. 20
D. 35

Correct Answer is b

39) A flashing red light at a railroad crossing means:

A. Stop, do not proceed until signals are completed
B. Slow down and proceed if clear
C. Proceed with caution
D. You have the right-of-way

Correct Answer is a

40) This green arrow on a lane use control signal means that:

A. You may use this lane
B. No traffic is allowed in this lane
C. You have the right-of-way
D. You must merge into this lane

Correct Answer is a

41) This sign with an orange background means:

A. Pedestrians ahead
B. End of construction zone
C. School crossing ahead
D. Flagger ahead

Correct Answer is d

42) This sign with an orange background means that:

A. A community service group is picking up trash along the highway ahead
B. Workers are on or very close to the road in the work zone ahead
C. Children are at play ahead
D. There is a pedestrian crosswalk ahead

Correct Answer is b

43) When an arrow panel in a work zone shows either of the following patterns, it means:

A. The bulbs on the sign are burned out
B. Drive with caution
C. Changes lanes immediately
D. Tune your radio to a station that gives traffic updates

44) The center lane in the illustration is used for:

A. Regular travel
B. Left turns only
C. Passing only
D. Emergency vehicles only

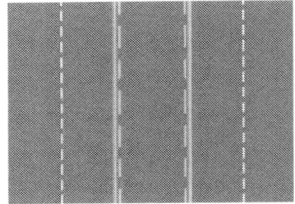

45) You may pass if the line dividing two lanes is a _____ line.

A. Broken white
B. Double solid yellow
C. Solid yellow
D. Solid white

46) Lanes of traffic moving in the same direction are divided by _____ lines.

    A.   Yellow
    B.   White
    C.   Red
    D.   Black

Correct Answer is b

47) You may not pass another car on either side of a _____ centerline.

    A.   Combination solid and broken yellow
    B.   Single broken yellow
    C.   Double solid yellow
    D.   Single broken white

Correct Answer is c

48) You may cross solid yellow lines:

    A.   To pass traffic moving in the same direction
    B.   During daylight hours only
    C.   At any time
    D.   When making turns

Correct Answer is d

49) The road edge on the right side is marked by a _____ line.

    A.   Broken white
    B.   Solid yellow
    C.   Solid white
    D.   Broken yellow audio

Correct Answer is c

50) Lanes of traffic moving in the opposite direction are divided by _____ lines.

    A.   White
    B.   Red
    C.   Black
    D.   Yellow

Correct Answer is d

51) When you see this black and yellow sign, it means:

    A.   The road to the right is for one-way traffic only
    B.   Detour to the right because of road construction
    C.   Slow down because the road ahead changes direction at an extreme angle
    D.   There is a crossroad ahead on your right

Correct Answer is c

52) When you see this sign with yellow background, it means:

A. There is an object on the roadway
B. Traffic is coming from the right
C. The road is curving sharply to the left
D. There is a merge point ahead

Correct Answer is c

53) At an intersection controlled by a stop sign, if you cannot get a good view of cross-street traffic when you stop behind the white top bar painted on the pavement, you should:

A. Wait 5 seconds, then proceed.
B. Sound your horn before proceeding
C. Put down your windows, listen for traffic, and then proceed
D. Pull forward slowly, check for traffic and pedestrians, and proceed when clear

Correct Answer is d

54) The posted speed limits show:

A. The minimum legal speed limit
B. The exact speed at which you must travel to avoid a ticket
C. The maximum safe speed under ideal road and weather conditions
D. The maximum safe speed under all road conditions

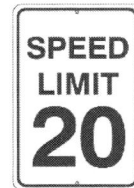

Correct Answer is c

55) A highway with two-way traffic is marked by which of these signs?

A. 1
B. 2
C. 3
D. 4

56) From the center lane, what maneuvers can you perform?

A. Make left turns
B. Make U-turns
C. Pass slower-moving traffic
D. All of the above

57) Which of these signs means that drivers should keep to the right?

A. 2
B. 1
C. 3
D. 4

KNOWLEDGE
Questions and Answers

1) What should drivers do if they see an emergency vehicle on the side of the road next to their lane of travel with lights flashing and/or sirens on?

a. Slow down by at least 20 mph for 1 mile.

b. Change lanes if safe and possible or, if not possible, slow down to a safe and prudent speed.

c. Ignore the vehicle and focus on driving.

d. Change lanes if safe and reduce vehicle speed by at least 20 mph hour.

Correct Answer is b. Change lanes if safe and possible or, if not possible, slow down to a safe and prudent speed.

2) Dangerous situations on mixed-use roads involve:

a. Parked cars

b. Distracted pedestrians

c. Drivers searching for their destinations and not paying attention.

d. All of the above.

Correct Answer is d. All of the above

3) Pedestrians have the right of way:

    a.   At street crossings

    b.   At any crosswalk whether marked or unmarked

    c.   If a driver is turning on a steady green or when making a right turn on red

    d.   All of the above

Correct Answer is d. All of the above

4) Distracted pedestrians are:

    a.   A small problem

    b.   A problem that is growing more serious annually

    c.   A problem that is becoming less significant every year

    d.   Not a problem

Correct Answer is b. A problem that is growing more serious annually

5) What percentage of pedestrians survive impact from a vehicle driving at 40 mph?

a. 90%

b. 50%

c. 10%

d. None of the above

Correct Answer is c. 10%

6) If a driver is convicted of a moving violation while holding a provisional license:

a. He/she is ineligible to convert to a full license until he/she has not been convicted of an offense for eighteen consecutive months.

b. He/she is no longer able to transport non-family members.

c. His/her provisional license will be suspended.

d. The person who co-signs the provisional license will also receive points on his/her record.

Correct Answer is c. His/her provisional license will be suspended.

7) If a driver needs to turn right at an intersection and the signal is red:

a.   The driver may turn right immediately.

b.   The driver may turn right after searching the intersection.

c.   The driver may turn right after coming to a complete stop, searching the intersection, and if a right turn on red is permitted.

d.   The driver must wait until the light turns green.

Correct Answer is c. The driver may turn right after coming to a complete stop, searching the intersection, and if a right turn on red is permitted.

8) What can a driver do from a shared left turn lane?

a.   Turn off or turn onto a multilane road.

b.   Pass other drivers who are blocking traffic.

c.   Drive for several miles until he/she finds an appropriate place to turn off.

d.   Make a right turn.

Correct Answer is a. Turn off or turn onto a multilane road.

9) If two vehicles arrive at an intersection that has stop signs on all four corners, which driver must yield?

    a.   The driver who is making a left turn across the travel path.

    b.   The driver who arrives first at an intersection.

    c.   The driver who is driving on a large public road.

    d.   The first driver to get to the intersection.

Correct Answer is b. The driver who arrives first at an intersection

10) A driver may pass another vehicle on a two lane road if:

    a.   There is a single broken yellow line between the two lanes.

    b.   There are two solid yellow lanes between the two lanes.

    c.   There is a solid yellow lane on his/her side of the road.

    d.   There is a double white line between two lanes of travel.

Correct Answer is a. There is a single broken yellow line between the two lanes.

11) A _____ can be used for both entering and exiting a highway.

a. Weave lane

b. Rumble strip

c. HOV lane

d. Passing lane

Correct Answer is a. Weave lane

12) According to the approved curriculum, which of these is good advice when driving near a motorcycle?

a. Always speed up to pass them.

b. Do not attempt to share a lane with a motorcycle.

c. Never allow a motorcycle to follow closely.

d. Always honk the horn when passing a motorcycle.

Correct Answer is b. Do not attempt to share a lane with a motorcycle.

13) Which of the following is true about large trucks and buses?

a. Large trucks and buses have a smaller blind spot than cars.

b. Large trucks and buses take less space to make a right turn.

c. Large trucks and buses have a shorter stopping distance.

d. Many people are killed in crashes involving large trucks or buses every year.

Correct Answer is d. Many people are killed in crashes involving large trucks or buses every year.

14) What are "No Zones"?

a. Areas that are off limits to passenger vehicles.

b. Lanes created especially for large trucks.

c. Areas of limited visibility around large trucks.

d. Areas that are reserved for official and emergency vehicles only.

Correct Answer is c. Areas of limited visibility around large trucks.

15) Which of the following is true about driving on bridges?

a. They can be crowded.

b. They often have limited visibility.

c. They usually have no shoulder that can be used for emergencies.

d. All of the above are true statements about bridges.

Correct Answer is d. All of the above are true statements about bridges.

16) When drivers enter an expressway in the acceleration lane they should:

a. Search for a gap in traffic and adjust speed to the speed of the traffic.

b. Set the cruise control for highway speed.

c. Stop and check traffic for a suitable gap.

d. Get as close to the vehicle ahead as possible so he/she can merge into the same gap.

Correct Answer is a. Search for a gap in traffic and adjust speed to the speed of the traffic.

17) Which of the following is true about speed limits on highways?

a. Law enforcement does not stop a driver unless a driver is going more than 10 mph over the speed limit.

b. Every interstate has a speed lane where you can go as faster than the posted speed limit.

c. Speed limits are limits you obey regardless of weather or road conditions.

d. Higher speeds contribute to more deaths and more severe injuries.

Correct Answer is d. Higher speeds contribute to more deaths and more severe injuries.

18) What is the safe procedure when driving in a tunnel?

a. Turn on lights and take off sunglasses.

b. Drive through as quickly as possible.

c. Turn off lights and put on sunglasses.

d. Turn on hazard lights when entering.

Correct Answer is a. Turn on lights and take off sunglasses.

19) Speed limits in work zones:

a. Change with traffic conditions.

b. Are usually reduced for worker safety.

c. Remain the same.

d. Increase to accommodate a higher volume of traffic.

Correct Answer is b. Are usually reduced for worker safety.

20) If an emergency vehicle is approaching from behind, a driver should:

a. Stop in his/her lane and allow the emergency vehicle to get around.

b. Move as close as possible to the edge of the road and allow the emergency vehicle to pass.

c. Flash lights to warn drivers ahead.

d. Call 911 to report the emergency vehicle.

Correct Answer is b. Move as close as possible to the edge of the road and allow the emergency vehicle to pass.

21) If a vehicle's accelerator fails, into which gear should a driver shift?

a. Park (P)

b. Reverse (R)

c. Neutral (N)

d. Drive (D)

Correct Answer is c. Neutral (N)

22) If drivers cause damage to an unattended vehicle, they should:

a. Attempt to locate the driver of the damaged vehicle.

b. Leave a note with the driver's contact information

c. Leave a note with the tag number of the vehicle.

d. All of the above are correct.

Correct Answer is d. All of the above are correct.

23) If a vehicle's engine fails (shuts off) what should the driver do with the brake?

a. Keep firm steady pressure on the brake.

b. Keep light pressure on the brake.

c. Press the brake every 3-4 seconds to avoid lock-up.

d. Do not touch the brake until the vehicle is on the side of the road and out of the path of travel.

Correct Answer is d. Do not touch the brake until the vehicle is on the side of the road and out of the path of travel.

24) Which of the following should drivers do if they have a tire blow out?

a. Brake hard.

b. Grip the steering wheel firmly to maintain control of the car.

c. Drive to the nearest service station.

d. Continue driving normally.

Correct Answer is b. Grip the steering wheel firmly to maintain control of the car.

25) When driving in fog:

a. Use low beam headlights.

b. Use high beam headlights for better visibility.

c. Use the horn at 10 second intervals.

d. Turn on the heat in your vehicle.

Correct Answer is a. Use low beam headlights.

26) When a vehicle is riding on a film of water it is called:

a. Lane surfing.

b. Hydroplaning.

c. Skimming.

d. Understeering.

Correct Answer is b. Hydroplaning.

27) When traveling on snowy roads, what adjustment should a driver make?

a. Increase speed to avoid emergency vehicles.

b. Flash headlights every 30 seconds to increase visibility.

c. Reduce speed to avoid problems with reduced traction.

d. Sound horn when approaching intersections.

Correct Answer is c. Reduce speed to avoid problems with reduced traction.

28) If a driver with a provisional license is convicted of a traffic offense:

a. He/she must wait an additional 18 months, offense free, before being allowed to be converted to a full license.

b. He/she is no longer able to transport non-family members.

c. His/her provisional license will be suspended.

d. The person who co-signed his/her license will also receive points on their record.

Correct Answer is a. He/she must wait an additional 18 months, offense free, before being allowed to converted to a full license.

29) If drivers have had to drive on the side of the road for a time and want to resume driving, they should

    a.   Brake hard.

    b.   Jerk the steering wheel to the left.

    c.   Ease off the accelerator and carefully steer back onto the roadway.

    d.   Push hard on the gas pedal to spin wheel.

Correct Answer is c. Ease off the accelerator and carefully steer back onto the roadway.

30) If a driver's vehicle hits anything but the driver fails to stop, it is called a:

    a.   Smash and grab.

    b.   Hit and run.

    c.   Rude and crude.

    d.   There is no special name for it.

Correct Answer is b. Hit and run.

31) According to the law, open containers are defined as _____ :

a.   Any open bottles of any liquid.

b.   Any alcoholic beverage that is not as originally packaged.

c.   Any open container, no matter what is in the container.

d.   None of the above.

Correct Answer is b. Any alcoholic beverage that is not as originally packaged.

32) For a driver under the age of 21, the maximum legal BAC (zero tolerance) is:

a.   Less than.02.

b.   Less than.05.

c.   Less than.07.

d.   Less than.08.

Correct Answer is a. Less than.02.
*Notice: maximum legal BAC can be different from state to other (.00 -.02

33) Implied consent means:

a. A driver has agreed to be tested for the presence of alcohol when driving.

b. A driver has agreed to be tested for the presence of illegal drugs when driving.

c. More severe penalties for refusing to be tested.

d. All of the above.

Correct Answer is d. All of the above.

34) Which groups can sanction for drinking and driving?

a. DMV and the school district where the driver attends school.

b. Court system and the DMV.

c. Court system and the school district where the driver attends school.

d. Only the DMV.

Correct Answer is b. Court system and the DMV.

35) The legal definition of aggressive driving is:

a. Being rude to law enforcement and other drivers when driving.

b. Being rude to law enforcement when given a citation.

c. Committing two moving violations at the same time.

d. Committing three moving violations at the same time.

Correct Answer is d. Committing three moving violations at the same time.

36) To avoid driving while impaired, a driver should not use:

a. Any medication that may limit his/her abilities.

b. Illegal drugs.

c. Prescription drugs.

d. Over-the-counter drugs.

Correct Answer is a. Any medication that may limit his/her abilities

37) How long do alcohol-related charges stay on a driver's record?

a. Two years

b. Five years

c. Ten years

d. Forever

Correct Answer is c. Ten years

*Notice: A DUI (driving under the influence) Stay on your driving record for 10 years, and it will stay on your criminal record permanently

38) A driver _____ be cited for drowsy driving.

a. Will

b. Could

c. Might

d. None of the above

Correct Answer is d. None of the above

39) A new driver under the age of 25 is required by law to practice night driving for at least _____ hours.

    a.   6

    b.   8

    c.   10

    d.   12

Correct Answer is c. 10

40) According to the Driver Education curriculum, if a driver consumes alcohol, he/she:

    a.   Should plan not to drive.

    b.   Should only drive during daylight hours.

    c.   Should eat plenty of food to absorb the excess alcohol.

    d.   Should monitor his/her BAC so that he/she know that he/she is safe.

Correct Answer is a. Should plan not to drive.

41) A red indicator light on a dashboard indicates:

a.   A serious vehicle malfunction that must be addressed immediately.

b.   A vehicle malfunction that should be addressed but is not urgent.

c.   A vehicle system that is operating.

d.   A minor vehicle malfunctions.

Correct Answer is a. A serious vehicle malfunction that must be addressed immediately.

42) How long do alcohol related charges stay on a criminal record?

a.   Two years

b.   Five to ten Years

c.   Until a driver renews his/her license

d.   Forever

Correct Answer is d. Forever

43) A driver may pass another vehicle safely when:

a.   There is a single broken yellow line between the two lanes.

b.   There are two solid yellow lanes between the two lanes.

c.   There is a solid yellow lane on his/her side of the road.

d.   There is a double white line between two lanes of travel.

Correct Answer is a. There is a single broken yellow line between the two lanes.

44) The purpose of a diamond-shaped yellow sign with black markings is:

a.   To guide drivers to rest areas.

b.   To warn of hazards ahead.

c.   To provide hazards ahead.

d.   To indicate a lower speed limit.

Correct Answer is b. To warn of hazards ahead.

45) A parking brake:

a. Can be called an emergency brake because it will always stop a vehicle if the brakes fail.

b. Is used to secure a vehicle only when parked on a steep incline.

c. Is used to secure a vehicle when parked.

d. Will not allow a vehicle to move if engaged.

Correct Answer is c. Is used to secure a vehicle when parked.

46) If two vehicles arrive at a four-way intersection at the same time, which driver must yield?

a. The driver who is making a left turn across the travel path.

b. The driver who arrives first at an intersection.

c. The driver who is driving on a large public road.

d. The driver on the right if both drivers arrive at the same time.

Correct Answer is a. The driver who is making a left turn across the travel path.

47) A yield sign:

a. Means a driver must stop before entering traffic.

b. Means a driver should give way to other drivers, pedestrians, or cyclists.

c. Means two roads are separating.

d. Is frequently found in residential neighborhoods.

Correct Answer is b. Means a driver should give way to other drivers, pedestrians, or cyclists.

48) If an emergency vehicle is approaching, a driver should:

a. Stop in his/her current lane and allow the emergency vehicle to pass.

b. Move as close as possible to the edge of the road and stop.

c. Flash vehicle's lights to warn drivers ahead.

d. Call 911 to report the emergency vehicle.

Correct Answer is b. Move as close as possible to the edge of the road and stop.

49) A driver can protect him/her self from impaired driving, by avoiding

a. Substances that may affect his/her abilities.

b. Illegal drugs.

c. Prescription drugs.

d. Over-the-counter drugs.

Correct Answer is a. Substances that may affect his/her abilities.

50) When traveling on snowy roads, what adjustments should a driver make?

a. Increase speed to avoid emergency vehicles.

b. Flash headlights every 30 seconds to increase visibility.

c. Reduce speed to avoid problems with reduced traction.

d. Sound horn when approaching intersections.

Correct Answer is c. Reduce speed to avoid problems with reduced traction.

51) When a vehicle is riding on a film of water it is known as:

a. Lane surfing.

b. Hydroplaning

c. Skimming.

d. Understeering.

Correct Answer is b. Hydroplaning

52) What can a driver do from a shared left turn lane?

a. Turn off or turn onto a multilane road.

b. Pass other drivers who are blocking traffic.

c. Drive for several miles until he/she finds an appropriate place to turn off

d. Make a right turn.

Correct Answer is a. Turn off or turn onto a multilane road.

53) To start a vehicle, a driver should have:

a. One foot on the accelerator and one foot on the brake.

b. One foot on the brake and the other on the dead pedal.

c. One foot on the accelerator and the parking brake engaged.

d. The parking brake engaged and both feet off all pedals.

Correct Answer is b. One foot on the brake and the other on the dead pedal.

54) What line is used to mark the right edge of a road?

a. Broken yellow line

b. Broken white line

c. Solid yellow line

d. Solid white line

Correct Answer is c. Solid yellow line

55) What should drivers do when they see a speed bump?

    a.   Maintain current speed.

    b.   Accelerate.

    c.   Brake.

    d.   Reduce speed to suggested limit.

Correct Answer is d. Reduce speed to suggested limit.

56) What is the most important thing to do before starting to drive a vehicle?

    a.   Lock the doors.

    b.   Check around the vehicle.

    c.   Put on the safety belt and put away electronics.

    d.   Make sure the gas tank is full.

Correct Answer is c. Put on the safety belt and put away electronics.

57) At a stop sign where there is no crosswalk or stop line, the vehicle should be stopped:

a. Before the back of the vehicle enters the intersection.

b. Before the front of the vehicle enters the intersection.

c. When the front of the vehicle is even with the stop sign.

d. Before the front of the vehicle is even with the stop sign.

58) What are the three rules for using turn signals?

a. Signal when changing lanes, 2. Signal when turning corners. 3. Make sure the signal turns off after the tum is completed.

b. Signal early 2. Signal continuously 3. Make sure the signal turns off after the turn is completed.

c. Signal when changing lanes, 2. Signal when turning corners. 3. Use arm signals only when it is raining.

d. All of the above.

59) Reaction time or distance is?

a. The distance traveled from the time your brain tells your foot to move from the accelerator to pushing on the brake pedal.

b. The distance traveled from the time your eye sees a hazard until the time your brain recognizes the hazard.

c. The distance it takes to stop your vehicle.

d. The distance you travel from the time you perceive a hazard until the vehicle comes to a stop.

Correct Answer is a. The distance traveled from the time your brain tells your foot to move from the accelerator to pushing on the brake pedal.

60) You may drive off a paved roadway to pass another vehicle:

a. If the shoulder is wide enough to accommodate your vehicle.

b. If the vehicle ahead of you is turning left.

c. Under no circumstances.

Correct Answer is c. Under no circumstances.

61) You are approaching a railroad crossing with no warning devices and you are unable to see 400 feet down the tracks in one direction. The speed limit is:

a.   15 mph.

b.   20 mph.

c.   25 mph.

Correct Answer is a. 15 mph.

62) When parking your vehicle parallel to the curb on a level street:

a.   Your front wheels must be turned toward the street.

b.   Your wheels must be within 18 inches of the curb.

c.   One of your rear wheels must touch the curb.

Correct Answer is b. Your wheels must be within 18 inches of the curb.

63) When you merge onto the freeway, your speed should be:

a. At or near the same speed as the traffic on the freeway.

b. 5 to 10 mph slower than the traffic on the freeway.

c. The posted speed limit for traffic on the freeway.

Correct Answer is a. At or near the same speed as the traffic on the freeway.

64) When you drive in foggy conditions, you should use your:

a. Fog lights only.

b. High beams.

c. Low beams.

Correct Answer is a. Fog lights only.

65) A school bus in the lane ahead of you is stopped and its red lights are flashing. You should:

a. Stop, then proceed when you think all of the children have exited the bus.

b. Slow to 25 mph and pass cautiously.

c. Stop as long as the red lights are flashing.

Correct Answer is C. Stop as long as the red lights are flashing.

66) "Basic speed law" says:

a. You should never drive faster than posted speed limits.

b. You should never drive faster than is safe for current conditions.

c. The maximum speed limit is 70 mph on certain freeways.

Correct Answer is b. You should never drive faster than is safe for current conditions.

67) You must notify the DMV how many days after selling your vehicle?

a. 5 days

b. 10 days

c. 15 days

Correct Answer is a. 5 days

68) Safe driving means you should always look ahead to where your vehicle will be in _____.

a. 5 to 10 seconds

b. 10 to 15 seconds

c. 15 to 20 seconds

Correct Answer is b. 10 to 15 seconds

69) You must signal continuously during the last _____ feet before a left turn.

    a.   50

    b.   75

    c.   100

Correct Answer is c. 100

70) Which of the following statements about blind spots is true?

    a.   They are eliminated if you have one outside mirror on each side of the vehicle.

    b.   Large trucks have bigger blind spots than most passenger vehicles.

    c.   Blind spots can be checked by looking in your rear-view mirrors.

Correct Answer is b. Large trucks have bigger blind spots than most passenger vehicles.

71) You have had a minor traffic collision with a parked vehicle, but you can't find the owner. You must:

    a.   Leave a note on the vehicle.

    b.   Report the accident without delay to the city police.

    c.   Both of the above.

Correct Answer is c. Both of the above.

72) Unless otherwise posted, the speed limit in a residential area is _____.

    a.   20 mph

    b.   25 mph

    c.   30 mph

Correct Answer is b. 25 mph

73) You may legally block an intersection:

a. When you entered the intersection on the green light.

b. During rush hour traffic.

c. Under no circumstances.

Correct Answer is c. Under no circumstances.

74) If you park uphill on a two-way street with no curb, your front wheels should be:

a. Turned to the left (toward the street)

b. Turned to the right (away from the street)

c. Parallel with the pavement.

Correct Answer is b. Turned to the right (away from the street).

75) A Class C driver's license allows you to drive:

a. A 3-axle vehicle if the gross vehicle weight is less than 6,000 pounds.

b. Any 3-axle vehicle regardless of the weight.

c. A vehicle pulling two trailers.

Correct Answer is a. A 3-axle vehicle if the gross vehicle weight is less than 6,000 pounds..

76) To make a left turn from a multi-lane one-way street onto a one-way street, you should start your turn from:

a. Any lane (as long as it is safe)

b. The lane closest to the left curb.

c. The lane in the center of the road.

Correct Answer is b. The lane closest to the left curb.

77) If you are involved in a traffic collision, you are required to complete and submit a written report (sr1) to the DMV:

    a.   Only if you or the other driver is injured.

    b.   If there is property damage more than $1,000 or if there are any injuries.

    c.   Only if you are at fault.

Correct Answer is b. If there is property damage more than $1,000 or if there are any injuries.

78) Roads are most slippery:

    a.   During a heavy downpour.

    b.   After it has been raining for a while.

    c.   The first rain after a dry spell.

Correct Answer is c. The first rain after a dry spell.

79) You may not park your vehicle:

a. On the side of the freeway in an emergency.

b. Next to a red painted curb.

c. Within 100 feet of an elementary school.

Correct Answer is b. Next to a red painted curb.

80) You must notify the DMV within five days if you:

a. Sell or transfer your vehicle.

b. Fail a smog test for your vehicle.

c. Get a new prescription for lenses or contacts.

Correct Answer is a. Sell or transfer your vehicle.

81) Two sets of solid, double yellow lines that are two or more feet apart:

a. May be crossed to enter or exit a private driveway.

b. May not be crossed for any reason.

c. Should be treated as a separate traffic lane.

Correct Answer is b. May not be crossed for any reason.

82) To make a right turn at an intersection, you should slow down and:

a. Move toward the left side of your lane.

b. Avoid driving in the bicycle lane.

c. Signal for 100 feet before turning.

Correct Answer is c. Signal for 100 feet before turning.

83) You are driving on a freeway with a posted 65 mph speed limit. The traffic is traveling at 70 mph. You may legally drive:

    a.   70 mph or faster to keep up with the speed of traffic.

    b.   Between 65 mph and 70 mph.

    c.   No faster than 65 mph.

Correct Answer is c. No faster than 65 mph.

84) It is illegal to park your vehicle:

    a.   In an unmarked crosswalk.

    b.   Within three feet of a private driveway.

    c.   In a bicycle lane.

Correct Answer is a. In an unmarked crosswalk.

85) The safest way to use cellular phones while driving is to:

a. Use hands-free devices so you can keep both hands on the steering wheel.

b. Keep your phone within easy reach so you will not need to take your eyes off the road.

c. Review the number before answering a call.

Correct Answer is a. Use hands-free devices so you can keep both hands on the steering wheel.

86) If you have a green light but traffic is blocking the intersection, you should:

a. Stay out of the intersection until traffic clears.

b. Enter the intersection and wait until traffic clears.

c. Merge into another lane and try to go around the traffic.

Correct Answer is a. Stay out of the intersection until traffic clears.

87) The proper way to make a right turn is to:

a. Signal and turn immediately.

b. Stop before entering the right lane and let all other traffic go first.

c. Slow down or stop, if necessary, and then make the turn.

Correct Answer is c. Slow down or stop, if necessary, and then make the turn.

88) You must obey instructions from school crossing guards:

a. At all times.

b. Only during school hours.

c. Unless you do not see any children present.

Correct Answer is a. At all times.

89) You encounter a dust storm while driving. You should immediately drive slower and turn on your:

a. Interior lights.

b. Parking lights.

c. Headlights.

Correct Answer is c. Headlights.

90) To pass another vehicle, you should:

a. Not assume the other driver will make space for you to return to your lane.

b. Assume the other driver will let you pass if you use your turn signal.

c. Assume the other driver will maintain a constant speed.

Correct Answer is a. Not assume the other driver will make space for you to return to your lane.

91) You are driving on a freeway with a posted 65 mph speed limit. Most of the other vehicles are traveling at 70 mph. You may legally drive:

a. 70 mph or faster to keep up with the speed of traffic.

b. Between 65 mph and 70 mph.

c. No faster than 65 mph.

Correct Answer is c. No faster than 65 mph.

92) If you drive faster than other vehicles on a road with one lane in each direction and continually pass the other cars, you will:

a. Get to your destination much faster and safer.

b. Increase your chances of an accident.

c. Help prevent traffic congestion.

Correct Answer is b. Increase your chances of an accident.

93) Which of these vehicles must always stop before crossing railroad tracks?

a. Tank trucks marked with hazardous materials placards.

b. Motor homes or pickup trucks towing a boat trailer.

c. Any vehicle with 3 or more axles or weighing more than 4,000 pounds.

Correct Answer is a. Tank trucks marked with hazardous materials placards.

94) You are driving on a one-way street. You may turn left onto another one-way street only if:

a. A sign permits the turn.

b. Traffic on the street moves to the right.

c. Traffic on the street moves to the left.

Correct Answer is c. Traffic on the street moves to the left.

95) A large truck is ahead of you and is turning right onto a street with two lanes in each direction. The truck:

    a.   May complete its turn in either of the two lanes.

    b.   May have to swing wide to complete the right turn.

    c.   Must always stay in the right lane while turning.

Correct Answer is b. May have to swing wide to complete the right turn.

96) You may cross a double yellow line to pass another vehicle if the yellow line next to:

    a.   The other side of the road is a solid line.

    b.   Your side of the road is a broken line.

    c.   The other side of the road is a broken line.

Correct Answer is b. Your side of the road is a broken line.

97) At intersections, crosswalks, and railroad crossings you should always:

a.   Stop, listen, and proceed cautiously.

b.   Look to the sides of your vehicle to see what is coming.

c.   Slowly pass vehicles that seem to be stopped for no reason.

Correct Answer is b. Look to the sides of your vehicle to see what is coming.

98) Driving defensively means that you:

a.   Always put one car length between you and the car ahead.

b.   Look only at the car in front of you while driving.

c.   Keep your eyes moving to look for possible hazards.

Correct Answer is c. Keep your eyes moving to look for possible hazards.

99) You are driving on the freeway. The vehicle in front of you is a large truck. You should drive:

a. Closely behind the truck in bad weather because the driver can see farther ahead.

b. Farther behind the truck than you would for a passenger vehicle.

c. No more than one car length behind the truck so the driver can see you.

Correct Answer is b. Farther behind the truck than you would for a passenger vehicle.

100) All of the following are dangerous to do while driving. Which of them is also illegal?

a. Listening to music through headphones that cover both ears.

b. Adjusting your outside mirrors.

c. Transporting an unrestrained animal inside the vehicle.

Correct Answer is a. Listening to music through headphones that cover both ears.

101) Always stop before crossing railroad tracks when:

a. You do not have room on the other side to completely cross the tracks.

b. The railroad crossing is located in a city or town that has frequent train traffic.

c. You transport two or more young children in a passenger vehicle.

Correct Answer is a. You do not have room on the other side to completely cross the tracks.

102) When you tailgate other drivers (drive close to their rear bumper):

a. You can frustrate the other drivers and make them angry.

b. Your actions cannot result in a traffic citation.

c. You help reduce traffic congestion.

Correct Answer is a. You can frustrate the other drivers and make them angry.

103) Should you always drive slower than other traffic?

a. No, you can block traffic when you drive too slowly.

b. Yes, it is a good defensive driving technique.

c. Yes, it is always safer than driving faster than other traffic.

Correct Answer is a. No, you can block traffic when you drive too slowly.

104) When you see a signal person at a road construction site you should obey his or her instructions:

a. Only if you see orange cones on the road ahead.

b. Unless they conflict with existing signs, signals, or laws.

c. At all times.

Correct Answer is c. At all times.

105) When are you allowed to drive in a bike lane?

a. During rush hour traffic if there are no bicyclists in the bike lane.

b. When you are within 200 feet of a cross street where you plan to turn right.

c. When you want to pass a driver ahead of you who is turning right.

Correct Answer is b. When you are within 200 feet of a cross street where you plan to turn right.

106) You approach a flashing yellow traffic signal at an intersection. The flashing yellow light means:

a. Stop before entering the intersection as long as you can do so safely.

b. Stop. Yield to all cross traffic before crossing the intersection.

c. Slow down and cross the intersection carefully.

Correct Answer is c. Slow down and cross the intersection carefully.

107) There is no crosswalk and you see a pedestrian crossing the lane ahead of you. You should:

    a.   Make eye contact and then pass him/her.

    b.   Slow down as you pass him/her.

    c.   Stop and let him/her finish crossing the street.

Correct Answer is c. Stop and let him/her finish crossing the street.

108) A solid yellow line next to a broken yellow line means that vehicles:

    a.   In both directions may pass.

    b.   Next to the broken line may pass.

    c.   Next to the solid line may pass.

Correct Answer is b. Next to the broken line may pass.

109) Pedestrians are required to:

a. Use crosswalks at intersections

b. Look in both directions before crossing the street

c. Observe and obey "walk" and don't walk" signals.

d. All the above.

Correct Answer is d. All the above.

110) If a policeman motions you to go through a red light, you:

a. Wait for a green light

b. Obey the police officer and go through the red light

c. Run over the police officer

d. Sound you horn after the light turns green to alert the officer

Correct Answer is b. Obey the police officer and go through the red light

111) Passing is prohibited:

a.   In a curve

b.   Within 100 feet of an intersection

c.   Solid yellow line is in your lane

d.   All of the above

Correct Answer is d. All of the above

112) State inspection of vehicles is required:

a.   Only on vehicles that are over 10 years old

b.   Every year

c.   Every two years

d.   Only when you buy a new car

Correct Answer is b. Every year

113) What shape is a stop sign?

a.   Rectangular

b.   Square

c.   Round

d.   Octagon

Correct Answer is d. Octagon

114) Unless posted otherwise, the speed limit on an open county highway is:

a.   70 mph

b.   65 mph

c.   60 mph

d.   55 mph

Correct Answer is d. 55 mph

115) When another vehicle is following you too closely, you should:

a. Press hard on your brakes

b. Get behind them and turn on your high beam lights

c. Tap your brakes gently, slow down and let them pass

d. Drive slowly and make sure they can't pass you

Correct Answer is c. Tap your brakes gently, slow down and let them pass

116) A funeral procession led by a funeral escort vehicle comes to an intersection where you are waiting. What do you do?

a. Proceed through when it is your turn

b. Yield the right of way to the procession when the lead car goes through

c. Try to beat it through the intersection

d. Let the lead vehicle go through, but, if an opening appears, go on through

Correct Answer is b. Yield the right of way to the procession when the lead car goes through

117) To make a right-hand turn at a red light, you:

a. Turn on your turn signal and turn

b. Turn right only after the light turns green

c. Yield the right of way to oncoming traffic, then turn right after the lane is clear

d. Turn on your hazard lights and turn right

Correct Answer is c. Yield the right of way to oncoming traffic, then turn right after the lane is clear

118) What is a no zone?

a. A no parking area

b. A one-way traffic area

c. A tractor trailers blind spots

d. An area designated for no motor vehicles

Correct Answer is c. A tractor trailers blind spots

119) Which of the following is not true?

a. Dim your headlights within 200 feet of oncoming vehicles

b. Use your parking lights only while parked

c. Dim your headlights within 200 feet of vehicle you are following

d. To avoid being blinded by oncoming lights, look toward the right edge of the roadway

Correct Answer is a. Dim your headlights within 200 feet of oncoming vehicles

120) To park downhill, your wheels should be turned:

a. Straight

b. Toward the curb

c. Away from the curb

d. None of the above

Correct Answer is b. Toward the curb

121) Parking is prohibited:

a. Within 15 feet of a fire hydrant

b. Within 50 feet of a crosswalk at an intersection

c. Within 30 feet of the nearest rail of a railroad crossing

d. All of the above

Correct Answer is a. Within 15 feet of a fire hydrant

122) You cannot pass safely unless:

a. You can see far enough ahead

b. You can return to your lane before meeting oncoming traffic

c. Your vehicle is capable of the speed necessary to pass

d. All of the above

Correct Answer is d. All of the above

123) When you enter an interstate highway, you should:

a. Stop on the entrance ramp and wait for an opening in traffic

b. Drive on the shoulder until you can enter traffic safely

c. Adjust your speed to meet a traffic gap, then merge at a safe speed

d. Follow the entrance ramp until merged as you have the right of way

Correct Answer is c. Adjust your speed to meet a traffic gap, then merge at a safe speed

124) When you enter a highway from a driveway or private road you should:

a. Yield to the vehicle on your left

b. Yield to the vehicle on your right

c. Yield to all vehicles approaching on the roadway

d. Turn on headlights and proceed quickly without yielding

Correct Answer is c. Yield to all vehicles approaching on the roadway

125) Pedestrians have the right of way:

a. At a red light

b. When walking their dog

c. When they are walking with a cane

d. When they are crossing an alleyway or driveway

Correct Answer is d. When they are crossing an alleyway or driveway

126) If you approach a school bus with its lights flashing on an undivided highway, you must stop within:

a. 50 feet

b. 40 feet

c. 30 feet

d. 20 feet

Correct Answer is d. 20 feet

127) Roads are most dangerous:

a. After it rains

b. While it is raining

c. When it begins to rain

d. All of the above

Correct Answer is c. When it begins to rain

128) The penalty for a first offense for driving under the influence of alcohol or drugs is:

a. 3 years in the state penitentiary and fined $3000 dollars

b. 6 months to 1 year in the county jail and fined $1000 dollars

c. 2 years in the county jail and fined $3000 dollars

d. 24 hours to 6 months in the county jail and fined $100 dollars

Correct Answer is d. 24 hours to 6 months in the county jail and fined $100 dollars

129) The most important reason for a vehicle inspection is:

a.   State law requires vehicle inspections

b.   Safety is the most important reason to inspect your vehicle

c.   To make sure your lights are working properly

d.   To check for over inflated tires

Correct Answer is b. Safety is the most important reason to inspect your vehicle

130) It's important during a trip to:

a.   Watch for pedestrians crossing

b.   Check brake fluid level

c.   Watch gauges for signs of trouble

d.   Make sure your signals are working properly

Correct Answer is c. Watch gauges for signs of trouble

131) Some key steering parts are:

a. Tires, rims, lug nuts

b. Leaf springs, bellows, eye bolt

c. Axle, control arm, pressure plate

d. Spindle, tie rod, drag link

Correct Answer is d. Spindle, tie rod, drag link

132) Name a suspension system defect:

a. Leaking shock absorbers

b. Under inflated tires

c. Loose lug nuts

d. Cracked brake cylinder

Correct Answer is a. Leaking shock absorbers

133) What three kinds of emergency equipment should you have?

a. Flashlight, tire gauge, tire inflation foam

b. First aid kit, bandage gauze, pain reliever

c. Fire extinguisher, spare electrical fuses, warning device

d. Exterior hazard light, cell phone, wheel chock

Correct Answer is c. Fire extinguisher, spare electrical fuses, warning device

134) What is the minimum tread depth for front tires?

a. 4/32 inch

b. 2/32 inch

c. 7/16 inch

d. 3/8 inch

Correct Answer is a. 4/32 inch

135) What is the minimum tread depth for other tires?

a. 4/32 inch

b. 2/32 inch

c. 7/16 inch

d. 3/8 inch

Correct Answer is b. 2/32 inch

136) What should wheel bearing seals be checked for?

a. Tightness

b. Leaking

c. Fluid level

d. Safety

Correct Answer is b. Leaking

137) Why should you back toward the driver's side?

a. State law requires backing toward the driver's side

b. Because it takes less time

c. Because you can see better

d. So, you won't have to look over your passenger

Correct Answer is c. Because you can see better

138) If your vehicle is stopped on a hill, how can you start moving without rolling back?

a. Place wheel chock under front wheel

b. Place wheel chock under rear wheel

c. Partly engage clutch before taking your foot off the brake

d. Use your parking brake

Correct Answer is c. Partly engage clutch before taking your foot off the brake

139) Why is it important to use a helper when you back up?

a. To help avoid blind spots

b. To watch for obstacles

c. To free the passenger side mirror

d. So, you will not have to do all of the work

Correct Answer is a. To help avoid blind spots

140) What are the two special conditions where you should downshift?

a. Before stopping and exiting a curve

b. Before starting off and driving uphill

c. Before shutting engine off and before exiting vehicle

d. Before starting down a hill and before entering a curve

Correct Answer is d. Before starting down a hill and before entering a curve

141) Retarders keep you from skidding when the road is slippery. True or false?

a. True

b. False

Correct Answer is b. False

142) How many seconds of driving time should you look ahead?

a. 10 to 12 seconds

b. 8-10 seconds

c. 12 to 15 seconds

d. 15-17 seconds

Correct Answer is c. 12 to 15 seconds

143) What are the two main things to look ahead for when you are driving?

    a.   Traffic and road conditions

    b.   Vehicles and stoplights

    c.   Disabled vehicles and obstacles

    d.   Curves and potholes

Correct Answer is a. Traffic and road conditions

144) What's the best way to see the sides and rear around your vehicle when you are driving?

    a.   Use your helper

    b.   Use your mirrors

    c.   Use your signals

    d.   Use your horn

Correct Answer is b. Use your mirrors

145) What does "communicating" mean in safe driving?

a. Using cell phones

b. Braking often

c. Using your horn

d. Signaling your intentions

Correct Answer is d. Signaling your intentions

146) What three factors add up to total stopping distance?

a. Stopping distance/ reaction distance/ perception distance

b. Vehicle distance/ stopping distance/ reaction distance

c. Braking distance/ obstacle distance/ stopping distance

d. Perception distance/ reaction distance/ braking distance

Correct Answer is d. Perception distance/ reaction distance/ braking distance

147) If you go twice as fast, how much will your stopping distance increase: twice or four times?

   a.   Twice

   b.   Four times

Correct Answer is b. Four times

148) Empty trucks have the best braking ability. True or false?

   a.   True

   b.   False

Correct Answer is b. False

149) What is "hydroplaning"?

a. Tires lose contact with road and have no traction

b. Turning steering wheel but vehicle does not turn

c. Braking but vehicle does not stop

d. Form of surfing

Correct Answer is a. Tires lose contact with road and have no traction

150) What is "black ice"?

a. Very hot slippery tar

b. Oil slick on the roadway

c. Snow on the roadway

d. Thin sheet of clear ice on roadway

Correct Answer is d. Thin sheet of clear ice on roadway

151) You should use low beams whenever you can. True or false?

a. True

b. False

Correct Answer is a. True

152) What should you do before you drive if you are drowsy?

a. Eat

b. Sleep

c. Drink coffee

d. Exercise

Correct Answer is b. Sleep

153) What effects can wet brakes cause?

a. Slower stopping speed ·

b. Hydroplaning

c. Brake wear

d. Lack of braking power

154) You can safely remove the radiator cap if the engine is not overheated. True or False?

a. True

b. False

155) What factors determine a "safe" speed when going down a long, steep downgrade?

    a.   Speed/ space /distance /perception

    b.   Reaction time/ distance /speed /vehicle size

    c.   Weight of vehicle /length of grade / steepness /road conditions /weather

    d.   Perception /reaction /speed of vehicle /stopping distance

Correct Answer is c. Weight of vehicle/ length of grade/ steepness/ road conditions/ weather

156) Why should you be in the proper gear before starting down a hill?

    a.   So, you can focus on braking

    b.   You may not be able to shift back into any gear and all braking effect will be lost

    c.   To maintain speed

    d.   So, you will not damage the transmission

Correct Answer is b. You may not be able to shift back into any gear and all braking effect will be lost

157) Describe the proper braking technique when going down a long, steep downgrade.

158) At night, if an oncoming vehicle fails to dim its high beams, look:

a.   Toward the center of the roadway

b.   Toward the right edge of your lane

c.   Toward the left edge of your lane

d.   Straight ahead in your lane

159) you must use your seat belt:

a. Unless you are riding in a vehicle built before 1978

b. Unless you are riding in a limousine

c. If failure to do so may result in a traffic ticket

d. Only when driving on a highway

Correct Answer is c. And failure to do so may result in a traffic ticket

160) Two sets of solid double yellow lines two feet or more apart:

a. May only be crossed to enter a private driveway

b. Should be treated like a solid wall and not be crossed

c. Denote a lane for beginning or ending left-hand turns

d. Denote a center turn lane

Correct Answer is b. Should be treated like a solid wall and not be crossed

161) If the road is wet and your car starts to skid, you should:

a. Slowly ease your foot off the gas pedal

b. Slow down by shifting to a lower gear

c. Slow down by pumping your brakes quickly and firmly

d. Slow down by shifting into neutral

Correct Answer is a. Slowly ease your foot off the gas pedal

162) Before getting out of your parked car on the traffic side of the street, you should:

a. Give an arm signal that you are exiting your vehicle

b. Turn on your left turn signal

c. Turn on your right turn signal

d. Check traffic approaching from behind

Correct Answer is d. Check traffic approaching from behind

163) What is a "hazard"?

a. Any road condition or user that is a possible danger

b. Any obstacle in the roadway

c. Anything that obstructs the roadway

d. A game of chance

Correct Answer is a. Any road condition or user that is a possible danger

164) Stopping is not always the safest thing to do in an emergency. True or false?

a. True

b. False

Correct Answer is a. True

165) You should go right instead of left around an obstacle if:

a.   You will avoid skidding

b.   You will avoid hydroplaning

c.   You will avoid drivers passing on the left

d.   You will avoid a head on collision

Correct Answer is c. You will avoid drivers passing on the left

166) What is an "escape ramp"?

a.   A highway exit in case you cannot change lanes

b.   Any highway exits

c.   An extra lane to pass slower traffic

d.   An exit at the bottom of a hill to slow you down and stop

Correct Answer is d. An exit at the bottom of a hill to slow you down and stop

167) If a tire blows out, you should put the brakes on hard to stop quickly. True or false?

    a.   True

    b.   False

Correct Answer is b. False

168) What is an important precaution to take at an accident scene to prevent a second accident?

    a.   Stop your vehicle immediately no matter which lane you are in

    b.   Stand in the middle of the lane and wave to oncoming traffic

    c.   Call your boss

    d.   Put out flares

Correct Answer is d. Put out flares

169) When using your extinguisher, should you get as close as possible to the fire?

a. Yes

b. No

Correct Answer is b. No

170) Which statement is true?

a. You can always trust other drivers to turn in the direction they are signaling

b. Drivers with rental trucks are often not used to driving a large vehicle and may be more dangerous

Correct Answer is b. Drivers with rental trucks are often not used to driving a large vehicle and may be more dangerous

171) Which of these statements is true?

a. You should use your high beams from 7 pm until 7 am

b. Most drivers are more alert at night than during the day

c. Many accidents occur between 12 am and 6 am

d. Hazards are easier to see at night

Correct Answer is c. Many accidents occur between 12 am and 6 am

172) What should you do when you see a hazard in the road in front of you?

a. Turn on your 4-way flashers to warn other drivers

b. Stop in the roadway, set out triangles and go to the back of your vehicle to flag down drivers

c. Stop quickly and exit the roadway if possible

d. Steer and counter-steer around the hazard

Correct Answer is a. Turn on your 4-way flashers to warn other drivers

173) You should use your horn:

a.   When changing lanes

b.   To help you avoid a collision

c.   When a car gets in your way

d.   To make a deer move away from the roadside

Correct Answer is b. To help you avoid a collision

174) Convex mirrors will:

a.   Show a wider view than flat mirrors

b.   Make objects appear closer than they actually are

c.   Make objects appear smaller than they actually are

d.   Make objects appear larger than they actually are

Correct Answer is a. Show a wider view than flat mirrors

175) What type of fire will water extinguish?

a. Tire

b. Gasoline

c. Diesel

d. Electrical

Correct Answer is a. Tire

176) Why is it important to shift gears properly?

a. To keep the engine at the proper temperature

b. To keep the radiator cool

c. To keep the oil flowing through the crankcase

d. To help maintain control of the vehicle

Correct Answer is d. To help maintain control of the vehicle

177) With low-beam headlights on, you can see:

    a.   250 feet ahead

    b.   200 feet ahead

    c.   150 feet ahead

    d.   300 feet ahead

Correct Answer is a. 250 feet ahead

178) Which of these conditions can produce a skid?

    a.   Over steering

    b.   Over braking

    c.   Driving too fast

    d.   All of the above

Correct Answer is d. All of the above

179) What should you do if you are being tailgated?

a. Slam on your brakes

b. Turn on your 4-way flashers

c. Increase following distance

d. Motion for the driver to pass

Correct Answer is c. Increase following distance

180) Which of the following is true when driving in cold weather?

a. Use anti-freeze in your windshield washer fluid

b. Use bleach on your tires to increase traction

c. If the temp is below freezing, the engine will not freeze

d. Exhaust leaks are not a concern

Correct Answer is a. Use anti-freeze in your windshield washer fluid

181) When drinking alcohol, what is affected first?

a. Judgment and self-control

b. Kidney control

c. Coordination

d. Muscle control

Correct Answer is a. Judgment and self-control

182) What should you do when driving through a construction zone?

a. Only reduce speed if you see a worker near the road

b. Watch for holes in the road and drop offs

c. Stop before entering, then proceed in low gear

d. Go as quickly as possible to avoid congestion

Correct Answer is b. Watch for holes in the road and drop offs

183) When your brakes are wet, it is very easy to:

a. Hydroplane if traveling faster than 30 mph

b. Hydroplane

c. Overheat your brakes

d. Jackknife the trailer

Correct Answer is d. Jackknife the trailer

184) If you are stopped on the shoulder of the road on a divided highway, you must:

a. Place reflective triangles or flares within 10 minutes of stopping

b. Flag down the next passing motorist and request assistance

c. Wait for road-side assistance

d. Turn off your vehicle

Correct Answer is a. Place reflective triangles or flares within 10 minutes of stopping

185) The maximum speed limit for a school bus on a highway is:

a. 50 mph

b. 55 mph

c. 45 mph

d. 65 mph

Correct Answer is b. 55 mph

186) Before entering a curve, you should:

a. Slow down to a safe speed and downshift before entering the curve

b. Up-shift and accelerate before entering the curve

c. Come to a stop before entering the curve

Correct Answer is a. Slow down to a safe speed and downshift before entering the curve

187) You must come to a full stop at railroad crossings:

a. Always

b. When carrying passengers or hazardous cargo

c. At night

d. If the crossing is unmarked

Correct Answer is b. When carrying passengers or hazardous cargo

188) How many hours must you wait before driving following your last period of eight consecutive hours off duty?

a. 6

b. 8

c. 10

d. 12

Correct Answer is c. 10

189) About _____ of all fatal crashes involve drinking drivers.

    a.   One-third

    b.   One-half

    c.   One-quarter

    d.   Two-thirds

Correct Answer is b. One-half

190) When you double your speed, it takes _____ times as much distance to stop your vehicle.

    a.   3

    b.   2

    c.   4

    d.   5

Correct Answer is c. 4

191) "Off tracking" is:

a. Driving on a dirt road

b. Passing on the right

c. Pulling onto the shoulder of the road

d. Trailer wheels following a different path. Then the tractor wheels

Correct Answer is d. Trailer wheels following a different path. Then the tractor wheels

192) How far ahead should you look while driving?

a. 1/8 mile.

b. 1/4 mile.

c. 1/2 mile.

d. 3/4 mile.

Correct Answer is b. 1/4 mile.

193) Which of these statements are true about downshifting?

a. When you downshift for a curve, you should do so before you enter the curve.

b. When you downshift for a hill, you should do so after you start down the grade.

c. When you downshift for a curve, you should do so after you enter the curve.

d. When you downshift for a curve, do so just after the curve.

Correct Answer is a. When you downshift for a curve, you should do so before you enter the curve.

194) Which fires can you put out with water?

a. Tire fires.

b. Fuel fires.

c. Electrical fires.

d. Chemical fires.

Correct Answer is a. Tire fires.

195) Brakes can get wet when you drive through a heavy rain. Wet brakes cause:

    a.   Wheel lockup.

    b.   Trailer jackknife.

    c.   Pulling to one side.

    d.   All the above.

Correct Answer is d. All the above.

196) Which of these is a good rule to follow when driving at night?

    a.   Always use your high beams at night.

    b.   Look directly at the oncoming headlights.

    c.   Keep your speed slow enough to stop within the range of your headlights.

    d.   Keep your instrument lights bright.

Correct Answer is c. Keep your speed slow enough to stop within the range of your headlights.

197) If you are being tailgated, you should:

a. Increase the space in front of your vehicle.

b. Flash your brake lights.

c. Speed up.

d. Signal the tailgater when it is safe to pass.

Correct Answer is a. Increase the space in front of your vehicle.

198) Which of these statements about staying alert is true?

a. A half hour break for coffee will do more to keep you alert than a half hour nap.

b. There are drugs that can overcome fatigue.

c. It is not possible to fall asleep while sitting up.

d. The only thing that can cure fatigue is sleep.

Correct Answer is d. The only thing that can cure fatigue is sleep.

199) How far should a driver look ahead of the vehicle?

a. 1-2 seconds.

b. 5-8 seconds.

c. 12-15 seconds.

d. 18-21 seconds.

Correct Answer is c. 12-15 seconds.

200) Which of these statements about drinking alcohol is true?

a. Some people aren't effected by drinking.

b. A few beers have the same effect on driving as a few shots of whiskey.

c. Coffee and fresh air can sober a person up.

d. If you drink alcohol fast enough, it will effect you less.

Correct Answer is b. A few beers has the same effect on driving as a few shots of whiskey.

201) As the blood alcohol concentration (bac) goes up, what happens?

a. The effects of alcohol decreases.

b. The drinker is always aware of increased effects.

c. The person is even more dangerous if allowed to drive.

d. The driver can sober up in less time.

Correct Answer is c. The person is even more dangerous if allowed to drive.

202) Driving under the influence of a drug which could make you drive unsafe is:

a. Permitted if it is prescribed by a doctor.

b. Against the law.

c. Permitted if it is a diet or cold medicine.

d. Easier if combined with a small amount of alcohol.

Correct Answer is b. Against the law.

203) If a vehicle goes into a front wheel skid while moving in a forward direction, it will:

a. Slide sideways and spin out.

b. Slide sideways somewhat, but not spin out.

c. Go straight ahead but will turn if you turn the steering wheel.

d. Go straight ahead even if the steering wheel is turned.

Correct Answer is d. Go straight ahead even if the steering wheel is turned.

204) The most common cause of serious vehicle skids is:

a. Driving too fast for road conditions.

b. Poorly adjusted brakes.

c. To much weight on the front axle.

d. Bad tires.

Correct Answer is a. Driving to fast for road conditions.

205) which of these statements about backing up a heavy vehicle is true?

a. If the trailer begins to drift, turn the top of the steering wheel in the opposite direction of the drift.

b. You should avoid backing whenever you can.

c. You should use a helper, he/she should use clear voice signals.

d. It is safer to back a vehicle than to drive forward.

Correct Answer is b. You should avoid backing whenever you can.

206) High beams should:

a. Be used whenever it is safe and legal to do so.

b. Be turned on when an oncoming driver does not dim his/her lights.

c. Be dimmed when you are within 100 feet of another vehicle.

d. Be used as sparingly as possible.

Correct Answer is a. Be used whenever it is safe and legal to do so.

207) Stab braking:

  a. Should never be used.

  b. Involves locking the wheels.

  c. Involves steady pressure on the brake pedal.

  d. Will not allow you to turn.

Correct Answer is b. Involves locking the wheels.

208) For the average person driving 55 mph on dry pavement, it will take about _____ to bring the vehicle to a stop.

  a. Twice the length of the vehicle.

  b. Half the length of a football field.

  c. The length of a football field.

  d. Sixty feet

Correct Answer is c. The length of a football field.

209) The parking brake should be tested while the vehicle is?

a. Parked.

b. Moving slowly.

c. Going down hill.

d. moving at least 30 mph.

Correct Answer is b. Moving slowly.

210) The vehicle in front of you has a red triangle with an orange center on the rear. What does this mean?

a. The vehicle is hauling hazardous materials.

b. It is a slow moving vehicle.

c. It has an over sized load.

d. The vehicle does not pay road use taxes.

Correct Answer is b. It is a slow moving vehicle.

211) What is a safety zone?

a. An empty space next to the freeway dividers

b. A space set aside for pedestrians

c. The median strip on a divided highway

d. A space around your vehicle that allows you to react to driving hazards

Correct Answer is b. A space set aside for pedestrians

212) When you are driving in traffic at night on a dimly lit street, you should:

a. Drive slowly enough so you can stop within the area lighted by your headlights

b. Turn on your high beam headlights to better see the vehicles directly ahead of you

c. Keep instrument lights bright to be more visible to other drivers

d. Use your emergency flashers to be more visible to other drivers

Correct Answer is a. Drive slowly enough so you can stop within the area lighted by your headlights

213) If a pedestrian is crossing the street at a corner without crosswalks, you should:

a. Take the right-of-way

b. Slow down and proceed with care

c. Let the person have the right-of-way

d. Stop four feet from the corner

Correct Answer is c. Let the person have the right-of-way

214) Animals may be transported in the back of a pickup truck only if:

a. The sides of the truck bed are at least 18 inches high

b. They are properly secured

c. The tailgate of the truck is closed

d. The driver has at least 3 years of driving experience

Correct Answer is b. They are properly secured

215) When you want to pass a large truck in the center of three lanes, it is best to pass:

a. Quickly on the left and move ahead of it

b. Very slowly on the left and move ahead of it

c. Very quickly on the right and move ahead of it

d. Very slowly on the right and stay in your lane

Correct Answer is a. Quickly on the left and move ahead of it

216) Most serious accidents happen at what time of day?

a. Morning

b. Afternoon

c. Twilight-darkness

d. Serious accidents happen at about the same rate throughout the day

Correct Answer is c. Twilight-darkness

217) What is the only effective way to reduce your blood alcohol content (bac)?

a. Drinking coffee

b. Exercising

c. Allow your body time to get rid of alcohol

d. Taking a cold shower

Correct Answer is c. Allow your body time to get rid of alcohol

218) Checking traffic behind you:

a. Is not a good idea, look ahead

b. Will help you if you are being followed

c. Is only good if you are slowing down

d. Should only be done if you intent to back up

Correct Answer is b. Will help you if you are being followed

219) Where should you start your U-turn on a street with two lanes in each direction?

    a.   Always use the center left turn lane

    b.   The left lane

    c.   The right lane

    d.   Any available lane

Correct Answer is b. The left lane

220) When you are driving in the left lane of a four-lane freeway and wish to exit on the right, you should:

    a.   Carefully cross all the lanes at one time

    b.   Accelerate so you travel faster than all other traffic on the highway

    c.   Slow before beginning each lane change

    d.   Change lanes one at a time until you are in the proper lane

Correct Answer is d. Change lanes one at a time until you are in the proper lane

221) Use your high-beam headlights at night:

a. As little as possible

b. Only on unlit streets

c. Whenever it is legal and safe

d. Always on a highway

222) If you have had several beers before driving, the effects of alcohol will be reduced only by:

a. Taking a cold shower

b. Waiting several hours

c. Drinking several cups of coffee

223) You may not double park:

a. Except while waiting in a car

b. Except when making a delivery

c. There are no exceptions

d. Unless your vehicle displays a parking placard

Correct Answer is c. There are no exceptions

224) You may legally park in front of a driveway:

a. Under no circumstances

b. As long as you are parked for no longer than 15 minutes

c. If the driveway is in front of your house

d. If the driveway belongs to your friends

Correct Answer is a. Under no circumstances

225) Before changing lanes on a multi-lane highway you should:

a.   Sound your horn

b.   Turn on your headlights

c.   Reduce your speed

d.   Check your mirrors and blind spots

Correct Answer is d. Check your mirrors and blind spots

226) What should you do if your vehicle hydroplanes?

a.   Start stab braking.

b.   Downshift immediately.

c.   Accelerate slightly.

d.   Release the accelerator.

Correct Answer is d. Release the accelerator.

227) If you must make a very quick stop, you should brake so you:

a. Can steer hard while braking hard.

b. Use the full power of the brakes and lock them up.

c. Stay in a straight line and can steer.

d. All the above.

Correct Answer is c. Stay in a straight line and can steer.

228) When you are on top of a hill and about to go down a steep grade, which statement is true?

a. Never downshift until you are going down the grade.

b. Always downshift to a gear lower than you came up the hill before starting down the grade.

c. Put the vehicle in neutral while going down the grade and use a very heavy pressure on the brake pedal.

d. Use a steady brake pressure before starting down the grade.

Correct Answer is b. Always downshift to a gear lower than you came up the hill before starting down the grade.

229) You are driving a vehicle with a light load, and traffic is moving at 35 mph in a 55 mph zone. The safest speed for your vehicle in this situation is:

a.   30 mph.

b.   35 mph.

c.   50 mph.

d.   25 mph.

Correct Answer is b. 35 mph.

230) Perception distance is?

a.   The distance traveled from the time your brain tells your feet to move from the accelerator until your foot is pushing the brake pedal.

b.   The distance traveled from the time your eyes see a hazard until the time your brain recognizes the hazard.

c.   The distance it takes to stop once the brakes are applied the time until perception is reached.

d.   None of the above.

Correct Answer is b. The distance traveled from the time your eyes see a hazard until the time your brain recognizes the hazard.

231) How far ahead should you look when you are driving?

a. One football field.

b. Two football fields.

c. 5 - 10 seconds.

d. 12 - 15 seconds.

Correct Answer is d. 12 - 15 seconds.

232) Doubling your speed has what effect on braking distance?

a. No difference in stopping distance.

b. Twice the speed = twice the stopping distance.

c. Twice the speed = four times the stopping distance.

d. Twice the speed = eight times the stopping distance.

Correct Answer is c. Twice the speed = four times the stopping distance.

233) Which of the following emergency items are you not required to have?

    a.   Fire extinguisher.

    b.   Spare fuses.

    c.   First aid kit.

    d.   Warning triangles.

Correct Answer is c. First aid kit.

234) Which of the following is a basic step to take after an accident?

    a.   Protect the area

    b.   Notify the authorities.

    c.   Care for the injured.

    d.   All of the above.

Correct Answer is d. All of the above.

235) The acronym "GVW" means?

a. Government vehicle weight.

b. Gross variable weight

c. Global vehicle weight

d. Gross vehicle weight.

Correct Answer is d. Gross vehicle weight.

236) What is the most important hand signal for a helper to use when you are backing up?

a. Slow down.

b. Pull forward.

c. Come straight back.

d. Stop.

Correct Answer is d. Stop.

237) A fire extinguisher with a crating is designed for:

a. Electrical fires and burning liquids only.

b. Only burning wood, paper, and cloth.

c. Burning liquids only.

d. All fires regardless of fuel.

Correct Answer is a. Electrical fires and burning liquids only.

238) You should always aim the fire extinguisher at the top of the flames so that the chemicals will fall on the fire.

a. True.

b. False.

Correct Answer is b. False.

239) How many classes of hazardous materials are there?

    a.   3.

    b.   6.

    c.   9.

    d.   12.

Correct Answer is c. 9.

240) You may drive off a paved roadway to pass another vehicle:

    a.   Closely behind the truck in bad weather because the driver can see farther ahead.

    b.   Farther behind the truck than you would for a passenger vehicle.

    c.   No more than one car length behind the truck so the driver can see you.

    d.   Under no circumstances

Correct Answer is d. Under no circumstances

241) Your blind spot is the area of the road:

a. Directly behind your vehicle

b. You see in your rearview mirror

c. You see in your side mirror

d. You cannot see without moving your head

Correct Answer is d.   You cannot see without moving your head

242) The "three-second rule" applies to the space _____ of your vehicle.

a. To the sides

b. Ahead

c. In back

d. All around

Correct Answer is b.   Ahead

243) To make a right turn you start in the right-hand lane and end in:

a. The left lane

b. The lane closest to the curb

c. Any lane available

d. The center lane

Correct Answer is b. The lane closest to the curb

244) If you exit a freeway with a ramp that curves downhill, you should:

a. Slow to the posted speed limit for the freeway

b. Wait until you enter the curve before braking

c. Slow to a safe speed before the curve

d. Accelerate before the curve to prevent oversteer

Correct Answer is c. Slow to a safe speed before the curve

245) When planning to pass other vehicles, you should:

a.   Assume they will maintain a constant speed

b.   Assume they will let you pass if you use your turn signal

c.   Not assume they will make space for you to return to your lane

d.   Assume they will start braking when they see you trying to pass

Correct Answer is c. Not assume they will make space for you to return to your lane

246) To avoid accidents, drivers should communicate with each other by:

a.   Signaling when changing lanes/direction, slowing down, or stopping

b.   Using their horns in emergencies and when really necessary

c.   Using emergency flashers/flares/signs as needed

d.   All of the above

Correct Answer is d. All of the above

247) You are permitted to use the unpaved shoulder of the road to pass to the right of a car if:

    a.   The car ahead is waiting to turn left

    b.   It should never be done

    c.   You are turning right at the next corner

    d.   You are riding a motorcycle

Correct Answer is b. It should never be done

248) Which of these is not a safe driving practice?

    a.   Maintaining a three-second following distance

    b.   Staring at the road ahead of your vehicle

    c.   Keeping your low beam lights on during bad weather

    d.   Keeping a space-cushion around the vehicle

Correct Answer is b. Staring at the road ahead of your vehicle

249) When you are waiting to make a left turn, you should give the right-of-way to vehicles coming from the opposite direction:

a. Until at least two vehicles have passed

b. Until dangerously close cars have passed

c. Until all of the cars have passed

d. Until your traffic signal starts changing to red, then you must make a turn even if there are vehicles in the intersection

Correct Answer is b. Until dangerously close cars have passed

250) It is best not to drive in the fog, but if you must do so, you should use:

a. Low-beam lights

b. High beam lights

c. Fog lights only

d. Windshield wipers

Correct Answer is a. Low-beam lights

251) Before turning left, the right-of-way should be given to oncoming cars:

a. Until most cars have passed

b. That are more than 500 ft away

c. Unless they are turning right

d. Until it is safe to turn

Correct Answer is d. Until it is safe to turn

252) What does a flashing yellow light mean?

a. Merging traffic

b. Proceed with caution

c. Pedestrian crossing

d. Come to a full stop

Correct Answer is b. Proceed with caution

253) If a car ahead of you has stopped at a crosswalk, you should:

a.   Stop and then proceed when safe

b.   Change lanes, look carefully, and pass

c.   Slow down, look both ways, and proceed

d.   Drive to the right edge of the road and stop

Correct Answer is a. Stop and then proceed when safe

254) When a yellow arrow comes on as you are about to turn from a dedicated left turn lane, you should:

a.   Stop and not turn under any circumstances

b.   Speed up to get through the intersection

c.   Be prepared to obey the next signal that appears

d.   Make a protected turn since you have the right-of-way over all vehicles and pedestrians

Correct Answer is c. Be prepared to obey the next signal that appears

255) you are at a red traffic signal. The traffic light turns green, but other vehicles are still in the intersection. You should:

a. Wait until the vehicles clear the intersection before entering

b. Move ahead only if you can go around the other vehicles safely

c. Enter the intersection and wait for traffic to clear

d. Honk your horn to warn other drivers of your presence and then enter the intersection

Correct Answer is a. Wait until the vehicles clear the intersection before entering

256) What should you do if a tire blows out while you are driving?

a. Hold your steering wheel tightly

b. Slowly release the gas pedal, if you must brake, do so gently

c. Bring the vehicle to a stop off the road, and change tire

d. All of the above

Correct Answer is d. All of the above

257) Which of these statements is true about motorcycles?

a.   Motorcycles are small and are less visible on the road

b.   Motorcycles may not share traffic lanes

c.   Motorcycles should be followed at a greater distance

d.   Motorcycles always have the right-of-way

Correct Answer is a. Motorcycles are small and are less visible on the road

258) Why should drivers and passengers adjust seat headrests in motor vehicles?

a.   It helps people relax, relieving the stress of driving

b.   It helps people avoid and reduce the severity of neck injuries

c.   It lets people maintain their hair styles

d.   Tired people can prop up their heads, helping them stay alert

Correct Answer is b. It helps people avoid and reduce the severity of neck injuries

259) If an oncoming vehicle has started to turn left in front of you:

a. Maintain your speed and take your right-of-way

b. Slow or stop your car to prevent an accident

c. Honk your horn to warn the other driver and maintain your speed

d. Accelerate so you can clear the dangerous area quicker

Correct Answer is b. Slow or stop your car to prevent an accident

260) The road surface is most slippery:

a. During a heavy rain or storm

b. Just after the rain

c. Just when it starts raining

d. During a light rain

Correct Answer is b. Just after the rain

261) A driver who is taking a non-prescription drug should

a. Read the labels on the drug before driving

b. Drink alcohol instead

c. Continue to drive

d. Drive only during daylight hours

Correct Answer is a. Read the labels on the drug before driving

262) If your driving privilege has been revoked, you may:

a. Drive only in an emergency

b. Still drive to and from work or school

c. Not drive in this state with any license or permit

d. Drive only in the presence of a licensed parent or guardian

Correct Answer is c. Not drive in this state with any license or permit

263) Which of the following substances can affect your ability to drive?

a. Tranquilizers, marijuana and sedatives

b. Cough syrups and cold tablets containing codeine or antihistamines

c. All of the above

Correct Answer is c. All of the above

264) Which of these are true of slippery roads?

a. Shaded areas may have hidden ice spots that freeze first/dry last

b. Bridges and overpasses usually freeze before roads do

c. Wet leaves cause slipping, and wet ice is slicker than ice alone

d. All of the above

Correct Answer is d. All of the above

265) Which of these driving skills are affected by the use of alcohol and/or drugs?

    a.   Alertness and concentration

    b.   Reaction time and coordination

    c.   All of the above are affected.

Correct Answer is c. All of the above are affected.

266) Which of these statements are true about driving and taking drugs?

    a.   Only illegal drugs can impair your driving

    b.   Even over-the-counter drugs can impair your driving

    c.   Any prescription drug is safe to use if you do not feel drowsy

    d.   All of the above

Correct Answer is b. Even over-the-counter drugs can impair your driving

267) When you pass into the oncoming traffic lane of a two-lane road, you should consider:

a. Your speed relative to others, and your ability to accelerate

b. How much clear space you need to pass, and how much you have

c. The speed and distance of oncoming traffic, and possible hazards

d. All of the above

Correct Answer is d. All of the above

268) When you cross railroad tracks in slow traffic you should:

a. Sound your horn as you are crossing the tracks

b. Stop on the tracks until your light turns green

c. Stop between the crossing gates in case they close

d. Wait until you can completely cross the tracks before you proceed

Correct Answer is d. Wait until you can completely cross the tracks before you proceed

269) Following closely behind another vehicle:

a. Helps you avoid other drivers' blind spots

b. Is a common cause of rear-end accidents

c. Increases fuel efficiency

d. Is part of the standard driving test

Correct Answer is b. Is a common cause of rear-end accidents

270) When you enter a freeway you should check traffic by using:

a. The inside and outside mirrors only

b. Only your rearview mirrors

c. All mirrors and turning your head

d. Only your left side-view mirror

Correct Answer is c. All mirrors and turning your head

271) When you approach a sharp curve in the road, you should:

a. Start braking as soon as you enter the curve

b. Start braking before you enter the curve

c. Accelerate into the curve and brake out of it

d. Accelerate through the whole curve to increase traction

Correct Answer is b. Start braking before you enter the curve

272) Teenage drivers are more likely to be involved in a crash when:

a. They are driving with their peer as a passenger

b. They are driving with adult passengers

c. They are driving with teenage passengers

d. They are driving without any passengers

Correct Answer is c. They are driving with teenage passengers

273) If your tires are not inflated to the pressure recommended by the manufacturer, it may cause:

a. Low gas mileage

b. Uneven tire wear

c. Improper steering

d. All of the above

Correct Answer is d. All of the above

274) A diamond-shaped sign is a:

a. Road hazard sign

b. Interstate route sign

c. School crossing sign

d. Speed limit sign

Correct Answer is a. Road hazard sign.

275) If the road is marked with a solid yellow line and a broken yellow line on your side, you may pass:

a. Only in an emergency

b. If you are on an expressway

c. If traffic is clear

d. Only at an intersection

Correct Answer is c. If traffic is clear

276) If you experience brake failure while driving, you should:

a. Downshift and look for an area to slow down and stop

b. Pump brake pedal quickly, if useless, pump released parking brake

c. Stop off the road if possible, and call for help

d. All of the above

Correct Answer is d. All of the above

277) When you hear a siren or see the flashing red light of an approaching emergency vehicle and you are not in an intersection, you should:

a. Drive slowly in the right lane until it has passed

b. Speed up so that you can stay ahead of it

c. Drive to the right edge of the road and stop

d. Choose any of the above options

Correct Answer is c. Drive to the right edge of the road and stop

278) A red and white triangular sign at an intersection means:

a. Slow down if an emergency vehicle is approaching

b. Look both ways as you cross the intersection

c. Always come to a full stop at the intersection

d. Slow down and be prepared to stop if necessary

Correct Answer is d. Slow down and be prepared to stop if necessary

279) Orange construction signs warn you:

a. Of workers and road equipment ahead

b. That there are driver services ahead

c. Of an accident ahead

d. That you will have to come to a complete stop shortly

Correct Answer is a. Of workers and road equipment ahead

280) Turn your front wheels toward the curb when you are parked:

a. Facing uphill

b. On a level road

c. Facing downhill

d. Next to a fire hydrant

Correct Answer is c. Facing downhill

281) When you park downhill and there is no curb, your front wheels must be turned:

a.   Towards the road

b.   Parallel to the road

c.   Towards the side of the road

d.   In the direction of traffic

Correct Answer is c. Towards the side of the road

282) When roads are slippery, you should:

a.   Decrease the distance you look ahead of your vehicle

b.   Stop and test the traction of your tires while going up hills

c.   Avoid making fast turns and fast stops

d.   Refrain from driving at all costs

Correct Answer is c. Avoid making fast turns and fast stops

283) You may drive across a sidewalk to:

a. Avoid driving over a speed bump

b. Enter or exit a driveway or alley

c. Make a U-turn

d. Pass a traffic jam

Correct Answer is b. Enter or exit a driveway or alley

284) Drivers who eat and drink while driving:

a. Have no driving errors

b. Have trouble driving slow

c. Are better drivers because they are not hungry

d. Have trouble controlling their vehicles

Correct Answer is d. Have trouble controlling their vehicles

285) If a pedestrian is in a crosswalk in the middle of a block:

a. The pedestrian has the right-of-way

b. The pedestrian must yield the right-of-way

c. Vehicles have the right-of-way, but drivers must legally take care for the pedestrian safety

d. Drivers must honk the horn approaching the crosswalk, to urge the pedestrian to cross faster

Correct Answer is a. The pedestrian has the right-of-way

286) When a traffic signal light is not working, you should:

a. Stop only if other vehicles are present

b. Slow down and stop if necessary

c. Stop and then continue driving when it is safe

d. Proceed through the intersection as usual

Correct Answer is c. Stop and then continue driving when it is safe

287) If you see orange construction signs and cones on a freeway, you must:

    a.   Change lanes and maintain your current speed

    b.   Be prepared for workers and equipment ahead

    c.   Slow down because the lane ends ahead

    d.   Speed up to avoid rubbernecking

Correct Answer is b. Be prepared for workers and equipment ahead

288) When may you legally drive around or under a railroad crossing gate?

    a.   Under no circumstances

    b.   When you can clearly see in both directions

    c.   When the gate does not seem to be working correctly

    d.   When you think you can drive through before it comes down

Correct Answer is a. Under no circumstances

289) If you need to slow down or stop when other drivers may not expect it, you should:

a.   Use your emergency brake

b.   Look over your shoulder for traffic in your blind spot

c.   Quickly tap your brake pedal a few times

d.   Get ready to blow your horn

Correct Answer is c. Quickly tap your brake pedal a few times

290) What are the colors of the sign that tells you the distance to the next exit of a highway?

a.   Yellow with black letters.

b.   Black with white letters.

c.   Red with white letters.

d.   Green with white letters.

Correct Answer is d. Green with white letters.

291) When you drive through an area where children are playing, you should expect them:

a. To know when it is safe to cross

b. To stop at the curb before crossing the street

c. To run in front of you without looking

d. Not to cross unless they are with an adult

Correct Answer is c. To run in front of your without looking

292) A car behind you begins to pass you. You should:

a. Maintain your speed so traffic will flow smoothly

b. Pull to the right and stop so he can pass

c. Slow down slightly and stay in your lane

d. Blow your horn to allow him to pass

Correct Answer is c. Slow down slightly and stay in your lane

293) You are in a large truck's blind spot if you:

a. Drive close to the large truck's left front wheel

b. Cannot see the truck driver in the truck's side mirrors

c. Follow no closer than ten feet behind the large truck

d. All of the above

Correct Answer is b. Cannot see the truck driver in the truck's side mirrors

294) A traffic light is red, but a police officer is telling you to go ahead anyway. What should you do?

a. Wait for the green light

b. Change lanes and drive slowly

c. Do as the officer tells you

d. Stop and wait for the officer to approach you

Correct Answer is c. Do as the officer tells you

295) You should always use your emergency flashers when:

a. You are double parked in a traffic lane

b. You are parked on the side of the road in heavy fog

c. Your vehicle has broken down on the roadway

d. You are driving at night and you feel tired

Correct Answer is c. Your vehicle has broken down on the roadway

296) When you enter traffic from a stop (e.g., pulling away from the curb), you:

a. Should drive slower than other traffic for 200 feet

b. Need a large enough gap to get up to the speed of traffic

c. Should wait for the first vehicle to pass, then pull into the lane

d. Should expect other drivers to make room for you to enter traffic

Correct Answer is b. Need a large enough gap to get up to the speed of traffic

297) You should look carefully for motorcycles before you change lanes because:

a. It is illegal for motorcycles to share traffic lanes

b. Their smaller size makes them harder to see

c. They always have the right-of-way at intersections

d. They always have the right-of-way on the highway

Correct Answer is b. Their smaller size makes them harder to see

298) A driver's left arm and hand are extended downward. This signal means the driver plans to:

a. Turn left

b. Turn right

c. Stop

d. Start up

Correct Answer is c. Stop

299) If a parking space is reserved for people with disabilities, a non-disabled person may park there:

a. Under no circumstances

b. For less than ten minutes

c. If unloading numerous items

d. If no other spaces are available

Correct Answer is a. Under no circumstances

300) You can still drive to and from work if your license is suspended.

a. True

b. False

Correct Answer is b. False

301) A driver should be _____ from the vehicle in front of him/her.

a. At least 2 seconds

b. At least 2 car lengths

c. At least 3 – 4 seconds

d. 3 – 4 car lengths

Correct Answer is c. At least 3 – 4 seconds

302) For a driver under the age of 21, the maximum legal BAC (zero tolerance) is:

a. Less than.02

b. Less than.05

c. Less than.07

d. Less than.08

Correct Answer is a. Less than.02

303) What is the first thing a driver should do after deciding to make a turn?

    a.   Stop when necessary

    b.   Signal at least 100 feet from turn

    c.   Slow down

    d.   Put down any electronic devices

Correct Answer is b. Signal at least 100 feet from turn.

304) The purpose of traffic signs is:

    a.   To direct, to decide and to stop drivers.

    b.   To observe, to direct and to guide drivers.

    c.   To stop, to warn, and to decide drivers.

    d.   To regulate, to warn, and to guide drivers.

Correct Answer is d. To regulate, to warn, and to guide drivers.

305) According to the law, who must wear a seat belt?

a.   Only passengers under 18 and the driver.

b.   Only front seat passengers and the driver.

c.   Only passengers under 21 and the driver.

d.   All passengers and the driver regardless of age or position in the vehicle.

Correct Answer is d. All passengers and the driver regardless of age or position in the vehicle.

We are reaching out to our happy readers:

A heartfelt thanks for choosing our book.

Would it be fine for you to leave us a review in Amazon.com?

It will take a minute to make us feel good that you are happy.

☆ ☆ ☆ ☆ ☆

WISHING YOU ALL THE BEST ON YOUR EXAM.

The Learner Editions Team

*For suggestions and remarks please leave us a message at **editionslegal@gmail.com**.

Made in the USA
Columbia, SC
02 December 2020